Russia

by Susan H. Gray

Content Adviser: Professor Sherry L. Field,
Department of Social Science Education, College of Education,
The University of Georgia

Reading Adviser: Dr. Linda D. Labbo,
Department of Reading Education, College of Education,
The University of Georgia

COMPASS POINT BOOKS

Minneapolis, Minnesota

FIRST REPORTS

Compass Point Books
3722 West 50th Street, #115
Minneapolis, MN 55410

Visit Compass Point Books on the Internet at *www.compasspointbooks.com* or e-mail your request to *custserv@compasspointbooks.com*.

Cover: Saint Basil's Cathedral and Red Square in Moscow, Russia

Photographs ©: Claudia Dhimitri/Viesti Collection, Inc., cover; Natalya Kaynova, 4, 30; TRIP/V. Kanashev, 5; AFP/Corbis, 6; XNR Productions, Inc., 7; TRIP/B. Turner, 8, 39; TRIP/J. Heath, 9; TRIP/M. Barlow, 10, 23; TRIP/Y. Varigin, 11; Charles McRae/Visuals Unlimited, 12; TRIP/V. Larionov, 13; Scott Swanson/Hulton Getty/Archive Photos, 14; Hulton Getty/Archive Photos, 15, 16, 32; Stringer/Hulton Getty/Archive Photos, 17; David Gray/Hulton Getty/Archive Photos, 40; Jeff Greenberg/Photophile, 18, 33; Gary Hachfeld, 19, 42; Dimitri Zhurkin, 21; TRIP/V. Kolpakov, 22; Svetlana Zhurkina, 24, 25, 38, 45; TRIP/A. Tjagny-Rjadno, 26; TRIP/F. Torrance, 27; Unicorn Stock Photos/Jeff Greenberg, 28, 35; Tatyana Yefimova, 29; Larisa Gerasimova, 31; TRIP/N. & J. Wiseman, 34; Reuters NewMedia, Inc./Corbis, 37; Photo Network/Jeff Greenberg, 41, 43.

Editors: E. Russell Primm and Emily J. Dolbear
Photo Researcher: Svetlana Zhurkina
Photo Selector: Catherine Neitge
Designer: Bradfordesign, Inc.

Library of Congress Cataloging-in-Publication Data
Gray, Susan Heinrichs.
   Russia / by Susan H. Gray.
      p. cm. — (First reports)
   ISBN 0-7565-0130-X (lib bdg.)
   1. Russia (Federation)—Juvenile literature. [1. Russia (Federation)] I. Title. II. Series.
   DK510.23 .G73 2001
   947—dc21 2001001458

Table of Contents

"Privyet!"

"*Privyet!* Hello, friend! Welcome to Russia!" You might hear this greeting if you visit Russia. Russia is the largest country in the world. It lies in the northern half of the globe.

▲ *Children in Moscow dress in warm clothes for a cold Russian winter.*

▲ *A village in the Arkhangelsk region of Russia*

Russia is the only country that stretches across two **continents**. A continent is one of Earth's seven great landmasses. Russia lies in Europe and Asia. Russia is so big that it has eleven **time zones**!

▲ *Children slide down an icy hill in Moscow.*

The Arctic Ocean lies to the north of Russia. The Baltic Sea in Europe is on the west. On the east, Russia borders the Pacific Ocean. Kazakhstan, Mongolia, and China lie to the south. Russia has borders with fourteen countries.

The capital city of Russia is Moscow. Moscow is also Russia's largest city. More than 8 million people live there.

A Land of Many Parts

The Ural Mountains run north to south in Russia. A huge, flat land lies east of these mountains. This part of Russia is called Siberia.

▲ *Map of Russia*

▲ *A volcano in Kamchatka*

Great mountains and volcanoes rise along eastern Siberia. These volcanoes are active. Most Russians live west of the Ural Mountains.

The Volga River flows west of the Urals. The Volga is the longest, deepest, and widest river in Europe.

Because so much land in Russia is flat, rainwater doesn't have a place to flow. Part of Russia, then, is made up of **swamps**. In the cold north, the swamps are frozen solid.

▲ *The sun sets over the docks in Nizhniy Novgorod, a large city along the Volga River.*

▲ *Lake Baikal is the deepest lake in the world.*

Southern Russia has good, rich soil. Most of the country's crops grow in southern and western Russia.
The deepest lake in the world lies in southern Russia. It is called Lake Baikal. In some places, this lake is more than 1 mile (1.6 kilometers) deep. Lake Baikal holds more fresh water than any other lake in the world.

Land of Forests and Tigers

Many kinds of plants and animals are found in Russia. Large forests cover much of Siberia. Northern Siberia is too cold and harsh for trees. Only small, scrubby plants grow there. Polar bears, arctic foxes, and reindeer live on this land.

▲ *Forests of birch trees cover much of the Russian landscape.*

Siberian tigers wander the forests of the southeast. At 650 pounds (295 kilograms), they are the biggest cats in the world. Baikal seals swim in the clear waters of Lake Baikal. These seals can live to be more than fifty years old!

▲ *Baikal seals sun themselves on rocks in Lake Baikal.*

▲ *Brown bears live in the Russian forests.*

Western Russia also has many forests. Bears, wolves, moose, deer, and squirrels live there. Russia also has dozens of state and national parks.

▲ *Members of the Russian royal family, the Romanovs, were murdered in 1918.*

The Romanov family ruled Russia from 1613 to 1917. A Russian ruler was called a **czar**. The Romanov family wanted to build Russia up into a great country. They made the Russian people work very hard and treated them badly.

After years of bad treatment, the people were angry. In 1917, they threw out the Romanovs. A year later, the Romanovs were murdered.

The people started a new political system called **Communism**. Vladimir Lenin was its leader.

Soon Lenin died. A ruler named Joseph Stalin took his place. Stalin was a cruel man. He had anyone who was against him killed.

▲ *Joseph Stalin, left, and Vladimir Lenin, in 1919*

Under Communism, the government owned everything. It owned the schools, the farms, and the factories.

Government leaders made all the plans for everybody. They told farmers what crops to grow. They told factory workers what products to make. They even told children what to be when they grew up.

◀ *A man operates a large machine in a government-owned factory in 1955.*

By 1991, many people were tired of this. Mikhail Gorbachev was Russia's leader at that time. He felt people needed to decide things for themselves. He helped the government change so that the people could run their own lives.

Today, the Russian people are making plans for themselves. Some have opened up new stores. Some are learning new jobs. Children are thinking about what to be when they grow up.

▲ *Mikhail Gorbachev, center, waves to the crowd during a march.*

What Is Russia Like Today?

Russia is nearly twice the size of the United States. It does not have as many people as the United States, however. Most Russians live in or near cities such as Moscow, St. Petersburg, or Irkutsk.

In the cities, most people live in very small apartments. Russian apartments have tiny kitchens. They

▲ *Nevsky Prospekt is a famous street in St. Petersburg.*

▲ *Russian families often live in small apartments.*

usually have one bathroom and one or two other rooms. Grandparents often live with their children and grandchildren.

Many families in Russia have a television set. Many Russians have washing machines and then hang the clothes outside to dry. Few people have computers at home. Most people who have computers live in Moscow.

Some people who live in the city own *dachas* away from town. A dacha is a country home and the land that goes with it.

Some dachas are big. Most dachas are small houses with tiny gardens. People spend weekends at their dachas. They grow vegetables there in the summer. They store the vegetables and eat them during the long winters.

In the country, most people live in houses in villages. Some houses are made of logs from nearby forests.

▲ *A Russian couple plants potatoes at their dacha.*

Country roads are quite poor. Some country houses are spread far apart. People must walk or ride horses to visit one another.

▲ *Kittens are popular pets for Russians who live in the cities.*

Many people in Russia keep pets. Russians who live in their own houses like large dogs to protect them. Cats and hamsters are popular pets for people who live in apartments.

The Longest Train Track

Most Russians do not own cars. For long trips, they usually take a train.

The longest single train track in the world is Russia's Trans-Siberian Railroad. This railroad runs almost 6,000 miles (9,600 kilometers) from Moscow to Vladivostok. The trip takes more than a week.

◄ *The Trans-Siberian Railroad has thousands of miles of track.*

▲ *Russians wait for the bus in Penza.*

Some cities have subway systems. Russians travel by bus too. Buses serve people in the city and run between towns and cities.

What Is There to Eat?

Most Russian children have a good breakfast in the morning. They may eat hot cereal, pancakes, eggs, or sandwiches with butter, cheese, and sausage. The tasty bread can be white or dark rye.

▲ *Russians eat many kinds of bread.*

The big meal of the day is usually eaten at 1 P.M. It often starts with a bowl of hot soup. Russians like to eat **borscht**. It is a soup made from beets. It is served with sour cream on top. The main course is meat or fish and some vegetables. Dessert might be fruit or chocolate.

▲ *A Russian family eats a hearty meal.*

▲ *A man serves tea using a samovar.*

After the meal, nearly everyone drinks tea. Russians drink tea whenever they get together. A large urn called a samovar is sometimes used to boil water for tea. Many people serve tea made from herbs they grow in their gardens. Russians also drink coffee, cocoa, milk, and soda.

In the evening, Russians have a small meal. They might have meat or fish and vegetables or pasta. Bread is served at almost every meal.

▲ *A Moscow café serves hot meals to those in a hurry.*

People in a hurry can have a hot meal at a café. Or they can buy a *pirozhok*. That's a small, fried or baked pie with a meat, fish, or potato filling.

Caviar is a well-known Russian food. It is the eggs of a fish called sturgeon. Caviar is very expensive. People all over the world enjoy caviar from Russia.

Russian Schools

Russian children start school when they are six years old. Most Russian schools are very good.

A class usually has about thirty students. A child often goes all the way through school with the same classmates. Students in a class have many years to become good friends.

▲ *A teacher works with a student at a middle school in Penza, in central Russia.*

To read Russian, children must learn the Cyrillic alphabet. It has thirty-three letters. Students also learn English, German, French, or Spanish.

▲ *Russian children learn the Cyrillic alphabet.*

▲ *Schoolchildren take a field trip to the countryside with their teacher.*

Russian children study music, art, and dance too. They know the music of Peter Tchaikovsky. They learn of great Russian ballet dancers, such as Anna Pavlova.

▲ *Yuri Gagarin was the first person to fly in space.*

Children also study Russia's proud history in space. They learn about Yuri Gagarin. He was the first man to fly in space.

They also learn about *Mir,* the Russian space station. *Mir* is the Russian word for "peace." This Russian space station was sent into orbit in 1986. *Mir* became a place where people lived in space for months at a time! In 2001, the International Space Station (ISS) replaced *Mir.*

Things to Do for Fun

▲ *A woman sells dolls based on fairy-tale characters.*

Russians like to go to plays, the ballet, and concerts. Movies cost too much for most people. Children with computers love to play games on them.

Children also like puppet shows. They are often based on Russian fairy tales. Children love the tales of the hump-backed pony, the snow maiden, and the fire

▲ *Russian children play hockey on the frozen Kamenka River.*

bird. In some cities, children can visit the circus year-round. In other cities, they go to see cats do tricks!

In the winter, snow covers much of Russia. Children ice-skate, play hockey, or throw snowballs.

They also go cross-country skiing. In the Urals and the mountains of east Siberia, people enjoy downhill skiing. In some places, they can ski down the sides of a volcano!

In the summer, Russian children like to play soccer and volleyball. Swimming is also a popular sport.

▲ *Sunbathers and swimmers enjoy the beach where the Kotorosl and Volga Rivers meet.*

Special Days in Russia

New Year's Eve is a huge holiday in Russia. On this day, families and friends give each other gifts and celebrate. People go out in the cold and snow, even late at night. They wish each other a happy new year.

Many people have New Year parties. Someone dresses up as Grandfather Frost. He is an old man with snowy white hair and a long beard who brings presents.

Soldier's Day is in February. It is a day to honor men, especially men in the army and navy. On this day, girls give small presents to the boys in their class. People also set off fireworks.

International Women's Day is a special holiday in March. This day is set aside to honor mothers, grand-mothers, wives, and sisters. Everyone gives flowers and candy to the women they know. Boys give small presents to the girls in their class.

▲ *Children play in front of a huge billboard and figure of Grandfather Frost in St. Petersburg.*

▲ *Russian women are given flowers and presents on International Women's Day.*

▲ *A Russian bride leaves flowers at the Tomb of the Unknown Soldier in Moscow.*

Russians also love weddings. A big wedding party may last for two days. The new couple usually visits a monument to war heroes. The bride leaves her flowers there. It is a way to honor those who died fighting for peace. People say this custom brings luck to the new couple.

Special Things to See

▲ *A Fabergé egg made in 1906*

Visitors to Russia can see many wonderful things. In museums, they see beautiful eggs made by Peter Carl Fabergé. He was a jeweler who lived many years ago. He made eggs of gold and **enamel**. He decorated his eggs with jewels and tiny paintings.

Tourists might also see nested dolls called *matryoshka*. These dolls pull apart in the middle. Inside each doll is a smaller doll. Some sets have more than twenty dolls!

▲ *A Russian woman sells matryoshka dolls on the street.*

▲ *A Russian church is filled with colorful icons.*

Visitors may go to some churches in Russia. The most famous church is Saint Basil's Cathedral in Moscow. The church is more than 400 years old. It has brightly painted, onion-shaped domes.

Many Russian churches have pic-tures of angels and saints called **icons**. They are decorated with gold, silver, and gems.

If you visit Russia, you will learn much more about this huge and interesting country and its people. Then as you leave, you might say, "*Da sveedanya!* Until we meet again! I enjoyed my visit to Russia."

▲ *On the island of Kizhi, a bike rider rests in front of the famous Transfiguration Cathedral, which was built of wood and no nails!*

Glossary

borscht—a soup made of beets and served with sour cream

Communism—a political system in which the government owns almost everything

continents—Earth's seven great landmasses

czar—a Russian ruler

enamel—paint that dries to a hard, shiny surface

icons—pictures of angels and saints

swamps—lands almost all covered with water

time zones—regions in which the same standard times are used

Did You Know?

- Two world-famous ballet companies are based in Russia: the Kirov Ballet of St. Petersburg and the Bolshoi Ballet of Moscow.

- The weather in Siberia can be very cold. In fact, temperatures as low as –90° Fahrenheit (–68° Celsius) have been recorded.

- Members of the Russian Orthodox Church celebrate Christmas on January 7.

- Russia has more than 50,000 state public libraries with more than 1 billion books.

At a Glance

Official name: Russian Federation

Capital: Moscow

Official language: Russian

National song: "The Patriotic Song"

Area: 6,592,850 square miles (17,075,482 square kilometers)

Highest point: Mount Elbrus, 18,510 feet (5,646 meters)

Lowest point: Coast of the Caspian Sea, –92 feet (–28 meters)

Population: 145,552,200 (2000 estimate)

Head of government: Prime minister

Money: Ruble

Important Dates

1147	Moscow is founded.
1237–1240	The Monguls conquer Russia.
1547	Ivan IV, known as Ivan the Terrible, becomes the first Russian ruler crowned czar.
1604–1613	Russia fights in a civil war.
1613	Michael Romanov becomes czar.
1703	St. Petersburg is founded.
1762	Catherine the Great comes to power.
1812	Napoleon attacks Russia and then withdraws.
1905	Japan beats Russia in the Russo-Japanese War.
1917	Communists take control of Russia.
1922	The Soviet Union is established.
1991	Communist rule ends. The Soviet Union breaks apart. Russia becomes an independent country again.
2000	Vladimir Putin becomes president of Russia.
2001	*Mir* is replaced by the International Space Station (ISS).

Want to Know More?

At the Library
Fowler, Allan. *Moscow.* Danbury, Conn.: Children's Press, 1999.
Harvey, Miles. *Look What Comes from Russia.* Danbury, Conn.:
    Franklin Watts, 1999.
Stanley, Diane. *Peter the Great.* New York: William Morrow, 1999.
Thoennes, Kristin. *Russia.* Countries of the World. Mankato, Minn.:
    Bridgestone Books, 2000.

On the Web
Mir Space Station
http://www.hq.nasa.gov/osf/mir/
For information about the Russian space station

The State Hermitage Museum
http://www.hermitagemuseum.org/html_En/index.html
For an online tour of this St. Petersburg museum

Through the Mail
Embassy of the Russian Federation
2650 Wisconsin Avenue, N.W.
Washington, DC 20007
To get information about Russia's culture

On the Road
Fleischer Museum
17207 North Perimeter Drive
Scottsdale, AZ 85255
480/585-3108
To view a collection of Russian Impressionist paintings

About the Author

Susan H. Gray holds bachelor's and master's degrees in zoology from the University of Arkansas in Fayetteville. She has taught classes in general biology, human anatomy, and physiology. She has also worked as a fresh-water biologist and scientific illustrator. In her twenty years as a writer, Susan H. Gray has covered many topics and written a variety of science books for children.